T0137529

TWO KORAN

THE HEARSAY KORAN & THE HOLY KORAN

HTAY LWIN OO

HOW DIFFERENT TEACHINGS ABOUT SOCILOGY AND HUMAN RIGHTS

iUniverse, Inc.
New York Bloomington

iUniverse books may be ordered through booksellers or by contacting:

iUniverse
1663 Liberty Drive
Bloomington, IN 47403
www.iuniverse.com
1-800-Authors (1-800-288-4677)

ISBN: 978-1-4401-3917-8 (sc)
ISBN: 978-1-4401-3918-5 (ebook)

Printed in the United States of America

iUniverse rev. date: 05/05/2009

CONTENTS

PREFACE

Both media and our educated Muslims acknowledge that Muslims are two groups and Moderated Muslims who are under the title of Islam and deal with non Muslims harmoniously, and that Islamic fundamentalists, instill the hostile mind to people, evict the women from human societies, follow own sects and killing the innocent people by terrorist activities.

This is absolutely wrong consideration because they are not the Islamic fundamentalists, they are only fatawamic fundamentalists. They love **The Hearsay Koran** more than **The Holy Koran**.

Our educated Muslims should not accept the title "Moderate Muslims" with joyful hearts by obeying the Hearsay Koran. If we are standing on this state "moderate," that means we are double standing people between non Muslims and fatawamic fundamentalists or we give artificial smile to non Muslims while being loyal to terrorists.

Moreover we cannot further the "peace process of the world", unless we stand firmly for the way of peace, and to do this we must be Islamic fundamentalists or followers of The Holy Koran.

I present that the pure Muslim and the Muslim those who are using the name of Islam but loyal their fore fathers' heritage or own sects. And I am ready to debate or discuss with anybody the presentation that contains the ideology in this book.

Htay Lwin Oo
Islamic Scholar

INTRODUCTION

Human Rights & Islam

This is an "Age of Rights" and the word "Rights" is echoed all over the world. Every human being loves and is eager to look for this word. But the Rights groups are frustrated on how to accept Muslim people rather than others. Even though some Rights Groups acknowledge that some of Moderated Muslims Groups are emerging out today, they can not overtake the Islamic fundamentalists. While they are trying to establish mutual understanding between Muslims, some of them are not patient with **Muslims' behaviors** and groan upon **the Islamic laws (Koran)** and **the Prophet Muhammad**. The effect of this kind of promotion widens the rift of understanding between what is "Rights" between Muslim and non Muslim.

The words "human rights" are spoken easily, but extremely difficult to carry out. If there is no internal revolution in the society, the job human rights can not be done, because the most people wants human rights not to practice themselves but to export their adorable culture to others freely, and they never think how their culture affect to others. On the other hands, even though many people those who human rights abused is their already practiced since many generations. Their practices are eroding their own rights but they still love their culture and defend it.

Under this circumstance, the good willing of human rights activists might be not only heavy criticized of both human rights abusers and those who abused but also fought back.

Especially in our Islam, the human rights abusers and those who abused are very harmony since very long times. The human rights abused innocent Muslims are not only completely bewitched by the clerics but also they believe that the books of the clerics' hand-made as the Holy Koran which their adorable books.

Two Koran

Most of the Rights Activists and non Muslims think that the laws (Sharia) that our Muslim obeying today are from the doctrinal of The Holy Koran. And also our Muslims boost that we are followers of only one Book, the Holy Koran. But when we consider thoroughly our accustomed or what we obeying are, we can figure out ourselves that we are followers of two books, the Holy Koran and the Hearsay Koran. One is from the Origin of Omniscient God (Allah), we just believe it to read with Arabic pronunciation; and other is from the fatawas makers' group (Olmah), we follow and obey it more than the Holy Koran. We mold our behaviors, life style, mood and every affairs according with our Hearsay Koran (fatawas). And we are not willing to accept heartily what The Holy Koran teaches us if it against our tradition.

The Hearsay Koran

Instead of the teaching of Holy Koran, we are forced or betrayed to follow the Hearsay Koran that the evil clerics created chapters as Holy Koran and propagate in Muslims societies.

The Hearsay Koran contains the full of verses which are from the Muslim clerics group (Olmah). Olmah inspires their evil cleric to make the verses and betray innocent Muslims to obey it. The Hearsay Koran is not only one book, there are many verses books and culture exported translations Korans are counted in it. But all these books are same ambition to-

(1) It guides the people into the way of war

(2) It brings the people out of light into utter darkness

(3) It guides the people to the wrong path.

How the Hearsay Koran exist

Even while the Prophet Muhammad was alive, the people those who were entering under the title of Islam but they did not wish abolish their heritage-culture used to deny the Holy Koran and ignore the laws of Holy Koran.

"And your people call it a lie, even though it is universal truth," (6:66)

In this verse the word "your" refers to "Prophet Muhammad's" and "it" refers to the Holy Koran. So, we can see clearly the moods of so called the followers of Prophet Muhammad at the time of His present. The so called followers or Arabs accused that the Holy Koran is a lie and they don't want to accept it. They wanted to maintain their old traditional and continue human rights abuse freely. But in that time, Prophet Muhammad and his faithfully disciples were very decisive to carry out their mission, so the traditionalists could not over take the laws of Holy Koran.

But after our Prophet Muhammad, his successors, Abu Bakar, Umar, Uthamam and Ali passed away; the power crazy dictators seized the Islamic title, monopolized the Islamic spoken affairs and created the **Hearsay Koran** by using some verses of Holy Koran and favoring their wishes.

It was very easy to produce the Hearsay Koran for them under following situations.

On one hand, even though many people those who convert to Islam, they are not willing to follow the laws of Holy Koran that orders to change their bad behaviors and revolt their inner minds. And they do not want to leave their old culture that is **total-**

ly wiped off women rights or women are only sex slaves for them.

On the other hand, the power crazy dictators when they seized the State power, they wanted to prolong their powers and create the monarchy that is not accepted in Islam, so they reincarnated their old culture and indulged the majority old traditionalists.

When the rulers and those who were ruled harmony each other, the brutal rulers raised the clerics as their lackeys and grass-root organizers to prolong their powers, so the clerics' board (that is not accepted in Islam) was rising out to produce **the Hearsay Koran**.

But they dared not to destroy or edit the Holy Koran, because of using the mane of Holy Koran, they can easily organize the people those who are under the name of Islam; and they can get the mass supporting of Muslims those who happy to accept the title of Islam but dare not to throw away their old accustomed practice.

Therefore the brutal leaders and the clerics use the name of Holy Koran and lured the innocent Muslims to read only pronunciation of Holy Koran and betrayed them to obey their handmade campaign or the Hearsay Koran (fatawas) as Holy Koran.

We can easily see this document in Book of *Muartda and Whashkath* **"I (Prophet Muhammad) left <u>tow things</u> for you, if you firm on them, you will not be on wrong ways. These are the Holy Koran and accustom of (mine)."** These are fabricated because they wanted to use the name of Prophet Muhammad to create the Hearsay Koran or their evil verses *Fatawas*. The power crazy leaders and their lackey clerics are using the name of Allah and Prophet Muhammad while they are producing their evil verses *fatawas* to lure the innocents.

The Prophet Muhammad never mentions about other books for His followers to obey them, he just mentions about the Holy Koran as doctrinal. He himself is the best symbol or example of how he demonstrates upon laws of the Holy Koran.

When he is about to leaves this world or in his last Haj he said *"I delivered <u>one thing</u> to you, if you firm and follow it, you are not going to be wrong. This is only the book of Allah (the Holy Koran)."* This document is recorded in book of Muslim (Hadith).

The Prophet Muhammad said he delivered or left <u>one thing</u> for his followers Muslim, but why the writers of *Muartda and Whashkath* changed the <u>two things</u> instead of one thing. This is very clear that they try to create another book like Koran and distribute amidst the innocent Muslims.

There had been many righteous and educated Muslims in every era, but they did not have chance to revolt the evil clerics because the evil clerics are lackeys of the rulers and they have powers and rights whatever they want to do. Very sometime the evil cleric board accuses the righteous persons as infidel or apostate and terminates them.

As our people those who had been thousands years under the monarchy and its lackeys clerics, is fixed firmly according with evil clerics' handmade fatawas or edicts of Hearsay Koran instated of the verses of Holy Koran, we are seasoned practice in the Hearsay Koran, and we are accustomed enough to deny the verses of Holy Koran that is our adorable Book just in mouths.

The Holy Koran

That we love to read and we very charismatic in it but most of our Muslims never thought to read to understand in it; and also our clerics prevent their followers from study thoroughly understandable in it by using various strategies. In that The Holy Koran contains the universal truth which is from the Origin of Omniscient God (Allah).

"And this Koran is not such as could be forged by

4

**those besides Allah, but it is a verification of that
which is before it and clear explanation of the
books, there is no doubt in it, from the Lord of the
worlds (10: 37).**

Allah inspires omniscience into The Prophet Muhammad' heart
(spiritual body) and he reveals it (2:97). The Prophet Muhammad
was rising out while the world was under the utter darkness aged.
And he was the master of internal revolution to bring the people
into light or fully human rights. He abolished the monarchy and
clerics class (monasticism) (57:27). He wipes off all roots of war by
obeying the laws of Holy Koran (8:61). All verses of Holy Koran aim
to peace for human beings. So all of war lords and militants from
the Arabs those who hated each other became brotherhood and
one united body by the power of Holy Koran within 23 years.

The Holy Koran itself says that-

**"Indeed! there has come to you light ad clear book from Allah;
with it Allah guides him who will follow His pleasure into the way
of peace and brings them out of utter darkness into light by His
will and guide them to the right path"** (5: 15, 16).

(1) It guides the people into the way of peace

(2) It brings the people out of utter darkness into light

(3) It guides the people to the right path.

Grass Roots of Hostile Moods

The evil clerics transformed the Holy Koran into Hearsay Koran in
their evil translations divert the teaching of the Holy Koran, so our
Muslims understand that the bad people are Jews and the deviators
are Christians. And we are inspired the hostile mood on others. We
can find this kind of teaching in the very first chapter of the Hearsay
Koran.

"Guide us to the Straight Way, the way of those on

whom You have bestowed Your Grace, not of those who earn Your Anger (those who are Jews) nor of those who went astray (those who are Christians)" (1: 6, 7).

We can see almost every commentary of the Koran like this addition or explanation in the blankets. They give bad name to other people or, bad simple. This is only insulation to them; this is not only hostile on them but also defames the reputation of Holy Koran and inspires the innocent people to hostile moods.

How the Holy Koran teaches the people

The Holy Koran teaches people to become the holy hearts owners or meek. It never teaches to insult on others. We can see these kinds of teachings at the very first verses of the Holy Koran Chapter 1-

"Guide us to the Straight Way, the way of those on whom You have bestowed Your Grace, not of those who earn Your Anger nor of those who went astray." (1: 6, 7)

This is very beautiful teaching, the Holy Koran teaches us how to pray (train own self); and we pray (train ourselves) to get the right way which like the saints got and not like the way of the evil one nor deviators. In these verses, the saints, evil one and deviators are parable, the saints are good one and the evil and the deviators are bad one.

We instigate ourselves to train our mind to become the good, meek, honest, justice, peace makers people, and not to become the hostile one, bad one, violators and deviators. The Holy Koran never refers that who is bad people and who is deviator, but just refers to own behaviors and practices.

The Holy Koran never accept the exaggerations like this, it clearly says

"Muslims, Jews, Christians and those who wash themselves, whoever believes in the Origin of Omniscient God (Allah), and the last day, and does good they shall have their reward from their Lord, and there is no fear for them, nor shall they grieve (2:62, 5: 69).

The Holy Koran and the Hearsay Koran are very different each other. We are taught of Holy Koran that whatever his/her religious title is doesn't matter, if he/she believe in God and do good deeds they are going to enter the paradise or Heaven. And The Holy Koran never teaches to accuse others that they are deviators or accused people.

HUMAN RIGHTS

As we ignore the real teaching of the Holy Koran, we are totally human right abused and very oppressed by the evil clerics.

> **"And as for those who reject Our communication, penalty shall affect them because they transgressed," (6: 49)**

Under the title of human right there are many sub titles. In this book, woman's right, individual's rights, right of life style and minority's right are considered how we are affected penalty because of obeying the Hearsay Koran instead of Holy Koran.

WOMAN RIGHTS IN ISLAM

The Prophet Muhammad was the first woman rights leader since the dark ages. What the Arab culture considers about women is worse than animal. Our Prophet Muhammad saves them form the hell. This point is clear from the Holy Koran

> **"When a female is announced to one of them his face becomes black and he is full of wrath. He hides himself from the people because of evil of that which is announced to him. Shall he keep it with disgrace or bury her in the earth? Now surely evil is what they judge. "** 16: 58, 59

We can see in these verses, how Arab culture is worse on women. They don't want daughters, and when they get daughters they felt very shameful, and even though he keeps his daughter, he is very unhappy. Sometimes they kill their daughters for their dignity.

The Prophet Muhammad revolted that kind of behavior, we can see this action **"Now surely evil is what they judge."**

If we are real followers of the Prophet Muhammad, we have to continue to do what our Prophet did but now we don't follow the Holy Koran and just follow Hearsay Koran.

In marriage

The Holy Koran says,

Man and woman have equal right to choice his/her spouse. Women are not property; they are human beings and have to have equal rights as men.

> **"O you who believe! It is not lawful for you that you should take women as heritage against their will, ..."** (4: 19)

The Holy Koran says that women are not heritage, they are human beings and they have a human being's hearts. The man (male, including father or guardian) can not go against a women's will in marriage affairs. The word "will" regards their feeling, sentiment, or choice of beloved one or boy friends. That means they have to have rights in going out into the human societies, otherwise they are put into room-hidden or house arrested lives. In this scenario, how can they look for their beloved one or boy friends? But-

The Hearsay Koran teaches us-

Woman does not have the freedom to follow her own heart or feeling. Her heart does not belong to her in marriage affair-

> **The marriage agreement can be made legal by just two words, when a person said to another before the witnesses "I will let you marry with my daughter (including her name)," and the other reply "Yes," if so the marriage agreement is done.** *Sharmi volume 2, p 374*

In this verse, where is the value of human being woman (daughter), whether she loves or doesn't love she has to marry the man whom her father proposed.

> There are many similar verses and many books (not Koran), we can find this kind of verse in *Arrlam Giri volume 2, p 270.*

According to these verses, not only do the father and the bridegroom not acknowledge about woman's feeling, but also the witnesses do not respect the woman's heart. And in this case the father recognizes his daughter as his heritage and the bridegroom also accepts the heritage that is given to him.

In this case, most of our fellows Muslims are obey the Hearsay Koran heartily. We don't know or we don't care how the Holy Koran says. We don't know that our behaviors are abusing the human rights; we just know that we love our accustomed religion that is thought of teaching of the Holy Koran, our adorable book. By obeying of these verses of Hearsay Koran, women are abused their right and we are also abused our right to think about our women (mother, daughter, sisters and beloved one).

In Divorce

Under the Hearsay Koran-

We seem to acknowledge women are just one-use love toys, because of we obey the following verses of the Hearsay Koran-

(a) **Only the husband has rights to divorce, when the husband divorces his wife, it is lawful, the wife does not have the right to refuse whether she likes or dislikes, agrees or disagrees. The wife does not have rights to divorce to her husband.** *DorRe Mokhata volume 1, p 215; Shahi Waykaya volume 2, p 72.*

(b) **When the husband just speaks from his mouth to his wife "I divorce you," then it is already divorce whether there are witness's present or not, whether his wife hears his words or not.** *Kanzuddakaeik p 116*

(c) **After one or two times the divorcing, the husband has the right to reunite. Whether the wife**

> **agrees or disagrees does not matter, he can still do it.** *Kuduri p 174*

Where are woman's rights in a system where whatever the husband wishes, the wife (woman) needs to obey whether she is willing or not.

The Holy Koran never teaches this animal style divorce, nor treats women as cattle. If the man (male) acts like this, the woman can act in equal response.

In this case, most of our fellows Muslims are obey the Hearsay Koran with joyful hearts. We don't know or we don't care how the Holy Koran says. We don't know that our behaviors are abusing the human rights; we just know that we love our accustomed religion that is thought the teaching of the Holy Koran, our adorable book.

By obeying of these verses of Hearsay Koran, women are abused their right and we are also abused our right to think about our women (mother, daughter, sisters and beloved one) those who are abandoned under the animal style edicts of divorce.

(Laws of Divorce in Islam need more explanation; I am going to write how the laws of Hearsay Koran and laws of Holy Koran for divorce are different).

In this case, the true teaching of The Holy Koran is

Women also have the same rights to divorce as the men have.

> **They (women) have rights similar to those against them in a just manner** (2:228).

This law clearly says that how they (women) are treated by their husbands in divorce cases, they have equal rights to do upon the husbands. Not just the men have the rights to divorce, women have rights to divorce when they don't want or they don't like their husbands.

14

Involvement in mass

The Holy Koran says,

The believers (women and men), must be involved in the mass prayer ceremonies. That means women have the right to be involved in the civil societies, they don't need to stay at home in a room-hidden system.

> **O! Believers, the call is made for prayer on Friday (mass prayer), then hasten to the remembrance of Allah and leave off traffic; (62: 9).**

But our acceptance of belief is different from the real teaching of the Holy Koran because of practicing of the verse of **the Hearsay Koran says-**

> **All women must establish their prayers alone. They can not be involved in mass prayer or go to mosques that involve mass prayer. If they do, these kinds of actions instill loathing.** *Haydaya volume 1, p 103; DorRe Mokhata volume 1, p 83; joultol nira p 60*

These verses of our Hearsay Koran absolutely wipe off not only the Muslims women's rights to participate in the mass prayer ceremonies or civil societies but also drive them out from their faiths. The Koran mentions *Arminu* for believers, men and women are invited to take part in the mass prayers but the verses of our Hearsay Koran acknowledge just the men are believers. That means women are not counted as believers.

Under these kinds of verses or religious edicts, millions of Muslim women are still living room-hidden or house arrested lives. We can find this kind of societies in Burma (especially in, my native Rakhine State), Bangladesh, India, Pakistan, Afghanistan and many parts of Islamic countries.

In reality, the Holy Koran says **only the adulterous**

are ordered to stay in the house, for the sake of the families' or relatives' pride or reputation (4:15).

The other ordinary women, modest women and owners of good behaviors are not ordered to stay in house as room-hidden lives. They can go outside, they can make business, they can look for education, they can visit any part of the world, and they can even go to another planet.

In this case, most of our fellows Muslims are obey the Hearsay Koran with joyful hearts. We don't know or we don't care how the Holy Koran says. We don't know that our behaviors are abusing the human rights; we just know that we love our accustomed religion that is thought the teaching of the Holy Koran, our adorable book.

By obeying of these verses of Hostile Koran, women are abused their right and we are also abused our right to think about our women (mother, daughter, sisters and beloved one) those who are evicted from the human society.

In Education & Leadership

The Holy Koran says,

There are many verses in the Holy Koran that state that education, and learning, researching, discovering and inventing are religious obligation for every Muslim. Among those verses there are some verses that stand out.

(1)He (Allah) taught human being with the pen. Taught human being what he/she knew not. (96: 4, 5)

In these verses "the pen" means "the educational tool" including school, learning centers, books which contain various knowledge, historical event or records, all of education promotional devices and so on. We (human being) are taught with all these tools. That is why we need to hunger for education to get knowledge. That is what Allah guides or makes the laws for human beings (man and woman).

> **(2)Are those who educated equal to those who educated not? Only the educated human will meditate.** (39: 9)

This verse says clearly that the educated one is not equal to uneducated one, that means the educated one can accepting the peace "Islam," thinking how the society may develop or advantage, the uneducated is blind in any sense, he can not reach right way. So we (man and woman) need to lean the education; otherwise we can not understand what Islam aim to, guide to and how we can serve our religious obligatory.

> **(3)Indeed in the past generations' histories, there is a lesson for men of understanding.** (12:111)

This verse urges to study about the historical events of the world. Unless we (man and woman) are not allowed to study the historical event of the world, how can we be men of understanding and how can we figure out about lesson that is reconsidered to bring new generation for future.

> **(4)Indeed there have been life styles before you; therefore travel in the earth and see what was the end of rejecters.** (3: 136)

This verse clearly says that all men and women are said to travel around the world to look for knowledge and study the other people's life style what is good and what is needed to rethink.

Mentioning above all are to learn the education, the Koran never forbids the woman. And not says "just reading the pronunciation of Arabic Koran" is education.

Anybody (man or woman) who has enough or more quality of mental, physical, educational, and experience is allowed to lead the societies or States or countries or worlds (6:166). Therefore if someone disagrees or dishonestly defines the verses of Koran, he/she is not real Muslim. But evil clerics are doing this job very frequently. And under their created-

The Hearsay Koran-

Women are not allowed to learn wider field of study, literature, history, art, science and so on. They are just allowed to learn the very limited literature to be able to write and read the names of the things which are at home.

> **Let the daughters to learn only to able to write necessary letter (message) and the names (lists) of the things at home.** *Bahistizewar volume 4, to guard the kids, article 30*

The very majority people under the name of Islam are very joyful accept this laws of the Hearsay Koran and force to practice in Islamic societies. Under these kinds of laws, the women are not allowed to go high school and so far away form the colleges and university.

On the other hand, the Indian continental descendants and many of Arabs and African descendants are followers of the Hearsay Koran and its maker evil clerics. In all of their Madarasas (so called religious schools) do not have the female students' class for higher education until today. Under their system, the women do not have right to know about religious affairs because their Madarasas don't allow to women students to become the religious graduated one (Molawi or Imammat).

On the other hand, there is no school for learning to understand Koran except Madarasa. That why they (women) do not have to chance to understand the Koran.

In this case, most of our fellows Muslims are obey the Hearsay Koran with joyful hearts. We don't know or we don't care how the Holy Koran says. We don't know that our behaviors are abusing the human rights; we just know that we love our accustomed religion that is thought the teaching of the Holy Koran, our adorable book.

By obeying of these verses of Hearsay Koran, women are abused their right and we are also abused our right to think about our women (mother, daughter, sisters and beloved one) those who are excluded from the learning centers.

Women are only sex slaves for the evil leaders

Our Muslims are the most unfortunate and the most betrayed people of the world. We got good leaders for just very short term once a long time; but most of time had been under the boot of evil leaders and their hand-pick clerics (grass roots organizers).

They use (but never obey) some verses which are translated favoring their wishes and instill our innocent Muslims. And then they ever create the war in human societies giving the reason of different sects and different religions.

Today we can see what they are doing in the world; they are organizing to innocent Muslims to fight on Jews and Christians. When this war is finished, they are going to create the war on Moderate Muslims.

We have many lessons from the past. One of the examples is, Mujahidin who fought pro-communist government in Afghanistan (both they and the government are under the title of Islam) and when the war was over in 1993, another group (Taliban) came out and fought the Mujahidin government, when the Taliban got the power 1996, they tried to create the war on Shia Muslims by killing several diplomats from Iran in 1998.

That is answer, the power crazy leaders and evil clerics never think about peace and how to create the peace process, they always think about how they have to create the war. Not only Afghanistan, we can see everywhere of the evil clerics' groups, or regimes rule by. They are always trying to create the war. The same example is Iran- Iraq war (1980-1988), Iraq invaded to Kuwait in 1990. They use their hand-pick cleric to instill the innocent to hostile minded.

Look on past and past, until the much resent years of after our Prophet passed away, among the four great successors of our Prophet; Omar, Uthamam and Ali were assassinated; the murderers were neither Jews nor Christians. They were under the title of Islam.

Our Holy Koran never teaches to create the war, just to prevent the war with Jihad. The Jihad means to prevent or struggle for stop the war and establish the peace (Islam) by scarifying our lives, our wealth and whatever our belonging to. Now they define the Jihad is the Holy War (to create the war). This is absolutely against the real meaning of Jihad.

If so, why they create the war? The answer is very clear. Because of they are not only power crazy leaders but also they are sex crazy and **they want our mothers, sisters, daughters, and beloved wives to be their sex slaves.**

My remark may make the readers of this books and Moderated Muslims to be wonderful, but you (the readers) should consider the two verses that how they explain them.

When in war time, they ignite the followers to go to front lines to fight the infidels by using the verse 2: 154

> **"And do not speak of those who are slain in Allah's way as dead; nay (they are) alive, but you do not perceive,"** (2: 154)

And some of similar verses are used to instigate our innocent Muslims minds and recruit the suicide bombers. (But evil clerics never go to their saying Allah's way).

And they use their favoring explaining for 4: 3

"And if you fear that you shall not be able to deal justly with the orphan, then marry the women of your choice, two or three or four; but if you fear that you shall not be able to deal justly, then only one or that your right hands posses." 4: 3

They give the explanation for this verse is very harmony with the explanations for the fighters recruit verses. Their explanation is, Muslims men are allowed to marry more than one wife under the circumstances especially in war times. When Muslims fighters are killed in the battle fields, and leave the widows and orphans, the rest Muslims men can marry the widows of their comrades or followers.

If we study thoroughly what they use for these two verses, that they urge us "go to war and be killed, don't worry about your mom, sisters, daughters and you wives, we promise, we are not going to abandon them; we will marry them according to the Koran (their interpretation) 4:3." They never go to war, and they are waiting to marry the rest widows.

They pretended themselves as the saints, but their deeds openly show us what their inside. They pretend to love the Muslims, but actually they create the war and they drive us to the killing field, we must be killed because of being fired or our own bomb-belts and we must leave mothers, sisters, daughters and beloved wives as their sleeping-mates.

They will take-care our women by using sex slaves as called second wife, third wife, and fourth wife and so on. And they are going to drive our women out from the lives of believers, put them into the room-hidden lives or house arrested.

Even though the Holy Koran never says like this (see the real meaning of 4:3 in Polygamy in Islam), most of our Muslims can not turn to the real meaning form the translation of Hearsay Koran. They dare not to think that their believing is logical or not. We have practiced enough and enraptured in it.

POLYGAMY IN ISLAM

According to the Holy Koran, all Prophets before our Prophet Muhammad of the world had wives and children (13: 38); There are many people those who marry more than one wife under any religion not only under the title of Islam. When in polygamy affair, those who except under the title of Islam do not use their Prophet's name Moses, Jesus, Buddha (Master of Kapila 38:49). But our Muslims are using so much the name of our Prophet when our men marry more than one wife. That shows our people are very cowardly to admit our own fault and try to refuge in the name of religion to cover up by wrong ways.

That's why; almost all people of the world (Muslims and non Muslims) think that Muslims men are allowed to marry to multiple wives in Islam.

If the Hearsay Koran was thrown into the trash-container, polygamy case was silent in Islam under any circumstance and the Holy Koran never encourages, urges or requests to marry more than one wife under any situation.

The power crazy leaders and their lackeys evil clerics want to occupy the many women as wives, they use the name of Holy Koran, they not only the monopoly the authority of Islamic societies, but also make the dishonestly translate the Holy Koran favoring their wishes or they transformed the Holy Koran into the Hearsay Koran.

In the Holy Koran, the real meaning for this verse is-

"**if you (men/ women) fear** that you shall not be

able to deal justly with the orphan, then <u>adopt</u> the women of your choice, two or three or four; but if you fear that you shall not be able to deal justly, then only one or that your right hands posses." 4:3

In this verse "four" is not maximum yet, the word "two or three or four," is going on counting, so someone he/she can take the responsible for their foods, dresses, shelter, education and future affair he/she can adopt many more than four. If he/she can not responsible at least has to adopt one until they reach the puberty (4:6).

But in the Hearsay Koran-

4:3 "And <u>if you (men) fear</u> that you shall not be able to deal justly with the orphan, then <u>marry</u> the women of your choice, two or three or four; but if you fear that you shall not be able to deal justly, then only one or that your right hands posses."

Even though they translate like this, they never follow the whole law of this verse; just follow the phrase "**<u>marry</u> the women of your choice, two or three or four.**" This is very dishonest act.

Many of our educated Muslims they themselves dare not to consider the words "*wa inn kheftom*" **<u>if you (both men and women) fear</u>** and "*Nakah*," **<u>marry or adopt</u>** and follow the translations of fatamaic fundamentalists. But they try to defense the criticize to polygamy in Islam by explaining "under the circumstance of war times, the men were killed and their wives were left, the rest men are said to marry the widows because the men are worrying about their children and their future lives." They give the historical record of Uhud war that killed 70 out of 700 Muslims men and many widows and orphans were left.

The evil clerics take opportunity to carry out this verse (their translation and explanation) for sex indulged minded. They are happy to create the war and send our innocent people to the battle field to be able to occupy our widows legally.

In 4: 3, if we translate the words *"wa inn kheftom"* as **if you fear** and *"Nakah,"* as **marry**, this will be contradict from 4:129 **"You will never be able to do perfect justice between wives even if it is your ardent desire."** These two verses are studied thoroughly, the former law **"then marry the women of your choice, two or three or four; but if you fear that you shall not be able to deal justly, then only one or that your right hands posses"** opens some expectation to be able to justly between wives; the later totally closes for expectation. These are double standing laws or dishonest. Such a double standing law is not from the Holy Koran (4: 82). It is surely from their created Hearsay Koran.

Under their translation, it not only the women rights are totally ignored, but also the women's feelings are not acknowledged because the words **"if you fear"** mean **"if you worry about them or if you sorrow for them,"** so you need to take the responsible their survival or future. From the words "if you fear," if "you" is just referred to men, only men can sorrow for the orphans, only men can worry for the orphan, women do not have right to sympathize nor right to worry for orphan. This is very injustice prejudice. These kinds of teachings are not from the Holy Koran. Women are also human being and they own their human sentiments (feelings), happy, unhappy, sorrow, sympathize, mercy, affectionate and upset.

And then, according to their translation, how the Koran solves for women, if many women died because of disasters, diseases or under some kinds of circumstance such as earthquake, Tsunami and so on and the men were much populace than women in the rest societies?

The makers of the Hearsay Koran do not have the right and logical answer for this question. And if someone ask them like this, they will accuse him/ her as traitors of Islam, because they don't really believe in the Holy Koran, they just believe in the Hearsay Koran or their indulge wishes translations.

The Arabic words "wa inn kheftom" in 4:3

Even though in Arabic Grammar *"Tom"* represent for plural male, it is used in generally for both gender. The words *wa inn kheftom* are not contained in just here, we can find these same words *wa inn kheftom* in 2: 239, 4: 35, 4: 101, 9: 28; all of these verses mention "If you (both men and women) fear." why they wish to understand for *wa inn kheftom* "if you (only men) fear" only in this verse? Their answer is because of the word *Nakah* is contained in this verse.

The Arabic words "Nakah"

If the word *Nakah* is translated as "marry," their translation "if you (men) fear" would be right but contradict the verse 4:129 and out of ideology from the Holy Koran 4:82, already mentioned above. But we need to be aware that *Nakah* does not means marry for always, it sometimes means "stay together or adopt," we can take out this meaning by considering its opposite word *Talaq* "divorce," general understood the meaning of *Talaq* is "breaking the marriage tied" (between men and women) but sometime this words *Talaq* use for "between human being (both gender each other)" when in this condition, we can not translate as "breaking the marriage tied" we have to translate as "apart from each other or left someone who stay together before" 49:25.

And then, our traditional understanding set up our brain to make sense *Nakah* for marry through "sexual relation." This is not right for always, because we can find the words "sexual relation" stand for *massa, fahesha* and other metaphorical words not stand for *Nakah*, moreover we can find that spouse (they already made married *Nakah*) without sexual relationship 2:236, spouse (they already made married *Nakah*) you do not go in (4:23). According to the 2:236 and 4:23 the couple those who have already married but not "sexual relationship" that means "shelter together or adopt" is clear. The translation for *Nakah* as "adopt" correspond with the word *wa inn kheftom* in 2: 239, 4: 35, 4:101, 9:28; all of these verses mention "If you (both men and women) fear."

So the real translation for 4:3 is "**if you (men/ women) fear that you shall not be able to deal justly with the orphan, then adopt the women of your choice, two or three or four; but if you fear that you shall not be able to deal justly, then only one or that your right hands posses."**

But in this case, most of our fellows Muslims are obey the Hearsay Koran heartily. They don't know or they don't care how the Holy Koran says. They don't know that their behaviors are abusing the human rights, they just know that they love their religion that is thought from the Holy Koran that is said their adorable book.

Punishment on women

There must be law for every crime, light or serious and very human being must be under the equal laws. But, the misunderstanding between husband and wife in the social affair is not the serious crime.

But our Muslim men always looking for the way how can they oppress on the women. Even the very small case, they try to exaggerate to oppress the women, and our culture exporters' translations are prejudice and translate another verse of Koran to abuse women's right or they transformed the Holy Koran into Hearsay Koran.

> **"Those on whose part your fear desertion, admonish them (women), and leave them alone in the sleeping-place, and beat them, then if they obey you do not seek a way against them"**(4:34)

Those translators are very poor educated about the words *Dharaba* and prejudice to translate the word ***Dharaba* as beat** in this verse. The word *Dharaba* not only means "beat" but also gives definition "**seek, compare, figure out the ways and so on,**" we can find easily this meaning in (2:273, 13:17, 4: 101).

When we consider the verses of Holy Koran, we can find another verse similar like this verse (4:34), that verse 4:15 shows, the situation is worse than 4:34. But it is not allowed to beat on women, if so why the translators want to seek way to be able to beat the women. The answer is very clear that the translators are under the shadow of their culture and they can not free from their old tradition.

> "**And as for those who are guilty of an indecency from among your women, call to witness against them four from among you; then if they bear witness confine them to the house until death takes them away or Allah <u>opens some ways for them</u>.**"
> (4:15)

When we consider in this case, the situation is worse than 4:34, but it is not allowed to beat women. They get the chance "Allah opens some ways for them," that means the mercy of Allah and declares the freedom form the house arrested, not means to kill, or to beat, or to oppress or prolong their house arrested lives.

If so, in the minor case in 4:34, it should not be translated as "**beat them;**" this kind of translations are not propagation of pure and polite religion, it is an only the brutal culture exportation by using the name of religion.

In this verse, the word *Dharaba* does not means "beat" is clear, because of the following sentence "**if they acquiesce, <u>you do not find a way against them</u>.**" That's why the word *Dharaba* in this verse means "seek way for," refers to reunite, separate, divorce, make agreement for different issue and so on to avoid the quarrelling, noising, contenting, and many chaos situations or domestic violence.

That is why, actually, the translation of the verse is **"Those on whose part your fear desertion, admonish them (women), and leave them alone in the sleeping-place, and <u>seek for them</u> then if they acquiesce you do not find a way against them"** (4:34)

The Holy Koran never teaches that to oppress on human beings each other. But in this case, most of our fellows Muslims are obey the Hearsay Koran heartily. They don't know or they don't care how the Holy Koran says. They don't know that their behaviors are abusing the human rights, they just know that they love their religion that is thought from the Holy Koran that is said their adorable book.

UNDER THE CULTURES' SHADES

Even though some educated Muslims (those who are very little percentage of world Muslims) eager to save the fellow innocents Muslims under the boots of evil leaders, and they can escape from all fatawas, but they can not consider with colorless vision to the verses of Holy Koran because they can not pass to beyond the cultures' shades which influences on them for past many generations. So the power of Hearsay Koran is prolong in Muslims' minds.

Life style

Most of our Muslim people think that pagan style Arab dressing and ancient Indian style dressing (long shirts, turban and beard) are Muslims' dressing for men and the whole body cover up dressing styles are Muslims women's dressing. Under this kind of culture wave, we are lured to misunderstanding on the words "the clothing that guards, that is the best (7: 26)," "let them wear their (women's) internal-garments over their bosoms (24:31)" and "let down their (women's) external-garments (33: 59)" from real senses.

The Holy Koran says

> 7:26 **"O children of Adam we have indeed sent down to you clothing to cover your shame, and beauty, and clothing that guard, that is the best. This is of communication of Allah that they may be meditating."**

The teaching of Holy Koran is very clear and very pure for every national (not only Arabs and Indian continental descendants), we are said to dress the clothes that have of cover up our shame, and beauty (look good) for the physical body. And to understand the words "to cover your shame" are needed to recognize regional practice regional practice eyes and era.

For example, if we are said "eat your food," how we understand the word 'food' is under the regional practice, for someone who is growing up from "rice eating countries," he/she is going to understand "the food" refers to "rice;" if someone who is growing up from "wheat" for him/ her the word "food" is wheat and in the same way "corn" "cassava plant (tapioca)" are understand for their main food countries. We can not monopoly for "food" means just "rice."

And for the spiritual body, we have to control our mind not to bad mood on others, that kind of dress is called the clothing that guard against evil. We need to constraint our minds to avoid doing, thinking, committing from the bad deeds and we need to train our mind to be meek and good moral. We should not define the words "clothing that guard" must be Arabs and Indian continental descendants' style long shirt, turbans, skull-cap for men and the whole body cover up clothes for women.

The Holy Koran never commands the ironic laws for dress about "long shirts, turban or skull-cap and beard" for men and the veils which cover up the whole body for women.

And also the Holy Koran never says about how to cut hair and beard, they are depending on personal life style, and if someone he love the beard, he can leave like this but should be cleanse, and if someone he doesn't want the beard he can shave it, this not a sin. For hair too, it is depending on personal wish, nobody can complain to others because of hair or beard. The Islamic title is not like same club such as army, so we don't need same uniform or under same life style.

And the word "beauty" mentions our dressing style should be look good in every society where own people live in.

But the Hearsay Koran says

> **Those who cutting or shaving beards are transgressors and commit the big sin.** *Amdadul Mofthi volume 1, p 261*

This is very absurd and ionic law for human society. But our people are more favor to the verses of this Hearsay Koran in this case, if someone (male) do not have the beard (except naturally didn't come out) or shaving or cutting the beard are said transgressors. In the same way, the man who doesn't wear turban or skull-cap and long shirt is said weak faith.

Under the Hearsay Koran, women are more constrained with the culture. The word from 7:26 "to cover your shame" is monopolized with the view of Arab, Iran or India culture style thought. Now, we can find many translations Koran are trying to their culture export to others that means they wish to monopoly the Islam or they transform the Holy Koran into Hearsay Koran.

The Holy Koran says

> **24:30, 31 "Say to the believing men that they cast down their look and guard their private parts; that is purer for them; surely Allah is Aware of what they do.**
>
> **And say to the believing women that they cast down their look and guard their private parts and not show off their ornaments except what appears thereof, and let them wear their <u>internal-garments</u> over <u>their bosoms</u>, and display their garments except to husbands or their fathers or the fathers of their husbands or their sons or the sons of their husbands or their brothers or their brothers' sons or their sisters' on or their women or their right**

> hands posses or the male servant not having pas-
> sion or the children who have not attained knowl-
> edge of what is hidden of women; <u>and let them not
> stride their feet so that what they hide of their gar-
> ments may be known;</u> "

In these verses not only to women are said to composure, but also men are said same words, but the different nature of physical structure women are said to dress under wear to cover their bosoms. But too old, or too young and under the condition of sick or injure are exempt (24:31, 60). This is not abuse the woman rights. All female human being in the polite world (Muslim women or non Muslim women) are dressing the under wear today.

The Hearsay Koran says-

> 24:30, 31 "Tell the believing men to lower their
> gaze (from looking at forbidden things), and pro-
> tect their private parts (from illegal sexual acts).
> That is purer for them; verily Allah is All-Aware of
> what they do.
>
> And tell the believing women to lower their gaze
> (from looking at forbidden things), and protect
> their private parts (from illegal sexual acts) and
> not to show off their <u>adornments except only that
> which is apparent (like both eyes for necessity to
> see the way, or outer palms of hands or one eye or
> dress like veil, gloves, head-cover, apron, etc.),</u> and
> to draw <u>their veil all over *Juyubihinna* (i.e. their
> bodies, faces, necks and bosoms),</u> and not to re-
> veal their adornments except to husbands or their
> fathers or their husband's fathers or their sons
> or their husband's sons or their brothers or their
> brothers' sons or their sisters' on or their <u>(Muslim)
> women (i.e. their sisters in Islam)</u> or the <u>(female)
> slaves</u> whom right hands posses or <u>the old male
> servant who lick vigor</u> or the small children who
> have no sense of feminine sex. And let them not

stamp their feet so as to reveal what they hide of their adornments, "

When we read the meaning of the Holy Koran and the Hearsay Koran, we may think the translations may be same, but study them thoroughly, these are very different.

(1)-**The Holy Koran says** that the women have to dress the internal-garments to cover up   the bosoms. That means to wear the under-wear to cover up the breasts. Every polite woman of the world can accept this reasonable law.

-**The Hearsay Koran says** the ironic laws that women have to dress the adornments like both eyes for necessity to see the way, or outer palms of hands or one eye or dress like veil, gloves, head-cover, apron, to over up their bodies, faces, necks and bosoms. Even most percent family member women of the evil clerics can not follow this law.

(2)–**The Holy Koran says** when the women need because of sick, injury, give birth or operation they can open up before their closed relatives, their family's nurses (**their right hands posses**) and physicians doctors (**the male servant not having passion**).

-**The Hearsay Koran says** when the women need because of sick, injury, give birth or operation they can open up before their closed relatives, the female slaves and the old male servant who lick vigor or the small children. This is very ionic law for women to hospitalize in emergency situations.

The culture exporters' clerics translate use two words from 24:31 (*bi khomorihinna* and *juyubihinna*) to exploit the law of Islam to make their culture revolution on others.

They translate the words ***khomo*** for head-coverings or veils without considering the word ***khomo***. In reality ***khomo*** means overwhelm on inner (mind or remember or sense). That's why the Holy Koran very often uses the **khomo** is alcoholic (intoxicate) which cover up the remember or memories or inner sense, not cover up the physical heads.

In this verse, the word **khomo** is used for cover up the women's breasts which are acknowledged as inner parts of women; physical bodies; the heads, the hands and the feet are not the inner parts of physical bodies. Therefore the word **khomo** should not be translated as head-coverings. The real meaning for this word and here is <u>internal-garments</u> because of other word "*joyub*" bosoms that exactly say which parts of body are needed to cover up with **khomo** <u>internal-garments</u>. This is for upper parts of the body, and the external-garments must be dress over the internal-garments 55:39, this going to be two-layers garments for women.

And then another lower part of body is needed to cover up with the garments which do not mention about what kind of clothes, but the word **wala yathribna** let not stride over (widen their steps, cross over) mentions that the garments which must cover up the lower part of body when not in cross over, or widen step quickly. It might be pent or trouser that is more cover up the lower part of body when in cross over. The Holy Koran never says that the clothes must be overwhelming the whole body from heads to toes.

For the external-garments,

The Holy Koran says-

> 33:59 **"O Prophet! Says your wives, your daughters and the women of the believers that they let down upon them their external-garments; this more proper, that they may be known, and thus they will not be given trouble..."**

When we study the two verses of Koran for women dresses (24: 31 and 33: 59), women are said to dress two layers. The first layer is cover up for inner parts of body and the second layer is for modest (by dressing shirt or smock). In here, the word *jalabus* from 33:59 does not mean the whole body completely covers up clothing except the eyes or one eye to see the way, it just means shirt or smock. Every woman (Muslims or non Muslims) are wearing the two layers clothing today except in the sexy clubs and swimming clubs. There is no ionic law for our Muslims women beyond the Holy Koran under the reason of culture.

But the Hearsay Koran says

> 33:59 **"O Prophet! Says your wives, your daughters and the women of the believers to draw their cloaks (veils) all over their bodies (i.e. screen themselves completely except eyes or one eye to see the way); this will be better, that they should be known (as free respectable women), so as not to be annoyed, ..."**

The culture exporters' clerics translate the word *jalabus* as **cloaks (veils)** that cover up the whole body "screen themselves completely except eyes or one eye to see the way." We can see how they hostile on women these two verses 24: 31 and 33:59. They translate the two words "*khomo*" and "*jalabus*" are same meaning "the whole body covers up clothes."

According to their translations, women have to dress two layers of the whole body covered up clothes and do not have to have under wears that cover up for inner parts of body. If so what is modest by covering up with the two layers clothes like blankets on the nicked body? That's why women are two folds trouble victims under the laws of Hearsay Koran. The first one is they have to have dress their body with two layers whole body cover up clothes whether hot or cold weather; and the second one is even they cover up like this, they don't have under wear to control their inner part so they feel some trouble. But most of our women are laying these kinds of laws, because no modest women can follow them.

Moreover the culture exporters don't care about the laws of Holy Koran and human beings women; they confirm their ionic law with their edicts-

> **"The women are not allowed to display before the stranger those are not closed relatives <u>even a hair</u>"** **"the young women should not display their faces nor stand publicly" it is big sin.** *DorRe Mokhata volume 2, p 242*

In life style, most of our fellows Muslims are psychologically forced to obey the Hearsay Koran heartily. They don't know or they don't care how the Holy Koran says. They don't know that their behaviors are abusing the human rights, they just know that they love their religion that is thought from the Holy Koran that is said their adorable book.

RIGHT TO BELIEVE

According to the Holy Koran, race, color, gender and belief is not an issue to be holy person. Every single person has right to believe according with his/her own wishes (18:29). The Holy Koran says that the most holy person is those who do peace only favoring the Origin of Omniscient God (Allah) without interesting his/her won benefits.

Jews, Christians or other non Muslims can not be hated because of their belief or religious titles. And the Holy Koran never inspires into the believers to fulfill anti-Jewish mined, anti-Christian minded or anti-non Muslims minded.

The Holy Koran teaches that the responsible of our Muslims are not only respect the other religions but also scarify our lives, wealth, and by all means to protect or revolt against destroyers of all kinds of worship places.

> "Permission (to revolt) is given to those upon whom war is made because they are oppressed, and most surely Allah is well able to assist them. Those who have been expelled from their homes without a just cause except that they say; Our Lord is Allah. And had there not been Allah's repelling some people by others, certainly there would have been pulled down monasteries and churches and synagogues and mosques in which Allah's name are much meditated; surely will help who helps His cause, (22: 39-40)."

How beautiful teachings in the Holy Koran, Synagogues represent for Jews, Churches represent for Christians, monasteries represents for Buddhists and Hindu and mosques represent for Muslims. In the Muslims majority country or community, when the extremists destroy such a worship place (Synagogues, Church or Monastery), our devoted Muslims must protest against them, or we have to do jihad (the struggling for revolution) against the destroyers because of the word (Allah's cause).

But most of our Muslims are very far from this teaching and hostile on non Muslims because we had been growing up under both Muslims powers crazy leaders and non Muslim dictators.

Among the Muslim leaders, there are many power crazy leaders who are dreaming to become the leader of Worldwide Muslims. So they used to sing the anti-Jewish and anti-western song to persuade the innocent Muslims hearts. On the other hands, they create "the evil clerics intelligent units" to instill anti- Jewish minded and anti-western minded into the innocent Muslims' sentiments by fabricating many myths (Hearsay Koran).

Under these kinds of regimes, all kinds of system (educational system, media system and every ways of propagation) are to aim to be hostile minded Muslims on non Muslims. Most of Muslims who grown up under these systems are practice enough to hostile on non Muslims because of their ideology is set up base on betrayed educational system.

And also, under some non Muslims dictatorship ruling countries, they said the world that they don't discriminate on Muslims, but their system is very clever; they never give or give very limited the educated Muslims rights to propagate, but they boost the evil Muslims clerics to fully chance to propagate their Hearsay Koran in Islamic societies.

When in long time, not only the fellow Muslims got practice enough to hostile minded to non- Muslims but also non Muslims' view point become Muslims are very stranger people of societies because of their different life styles. The consequence of this scenario sparks the religious riots among the Muslims and non Muslims.

In their policy, if the countries are in the chaos, they easily deny the Democracy or they can create the fake democracy countries by fraud the votes.

Individual Right or Right to thinks

The people who want the individual rights he/ she dare to consider thoroughly his/her heritage customs or faiths form the parents. Or he or she has to dare to revolt the obsolete traditions or heritages. The Holy Koran does not support to follow the heritage tradition of parents which is against the human moral code. If he/she dares not to revolt the old and obsolete tradition which is obstacle of the way of peace, or he/she blindly follows the traditional faiths, he/she can not reach the goal of individual rights.

> **"And when it is said to them, follow what Allah has revealed, they say: Nay! We follow what we found our fathers upon. What! And though their fathers had no sense at all, nor did they follow the right way."** (2: 170)

However the Holy Koran encourages considering accustoms from the parents, our Muslims generations are physical and psychological forced by the fatawas makers to follow the old traditional faiths without consideration.

The Holy Koran gives the full individual right to believe. The decision what he/she believe in can be made by oneself. Nobody can intervene in his/her belief.

> **"The truth is from your Lord, so let him who please believes, let him who please disbelieve."** (18:29)

Even we got such a beautiful law; our Muslims' hearts can not accept honestly this verse under the shadowing of the Hearsay Koran since many generations.

The brutal rulers own very good qualification to raise the thugs and selfish exploiters who favor to rulers and exploit to innocent people. And they know well the weak points of the innocents and use the ionic laws (which against the Holy Koran 2: 256) to prolong their powers.

The Muslim innocent people very love their faith (monotheism); they defense their faith by scarifying their lives. And also they very love their Prophet Muhammad who saves from their wrong faith in the past, and delivers the guidance (the Holy Koran). So they dare to die for their faith anytime.

The brutal rulers systematically use this point to penetrate into the Muslim innocent people. They created the evil clerics missions and gave well-train them how to control the Islamic societies. The evil clerics, lackeys of brutal rulers received proposal (money and others) from the brutal rulers and produce many books (Hearsay Koran), build many so- called mosques, their propagation centers (9:106) and betray the people.

In their books, they ever not only eulogize about he Holy Koran (just name) and they take their useful verses, or phrases out and mix with their edicts, but also praise about the Prophet Muhammad's name and they use his mane whatever they do with their own indulge minded.

Educated persons are very small percentage in every society and others very most people are really innocents who do not have enough education and knowledge to analyst (consideration). So the evil clerics can easily bewitch the majority because of under the name of Holy Koran and Prophet Muhammad and their powers because they seized the state power. They persuade some people and give the authority to act among the societies and create the intelligent cells to eradicate the educated branches.

The evil regimes systematically instill the people to accept their edicts (Hearsay Koran) as the commands of Allah and practice of Prophet Muhammad, and if someone criticizes their edicts (so people thought verses of Holy Koran), he is going to be killed.

> **If someone accidentally leaves from <u>his belief Is-</u><u>lam</u>, give him three days to rethink; if he does not come back to Islam, he is going to be killed.** *Arrlam Giri volume 2, p 876; Fatawa hi diyat volume 2, p 877*

Under these kinds of edicts, the innocent people totally lost their exits asking to about woman rights, educational rights, and their own thinking rights. Because in this edict, the words "his belief Islam" not refers to the verses of Holy Koran, just refers to the laws of edict, called **Akidah,** some of them are totally against the Holy Koran, and how to accept the **Akidah** is depending on sects.

In the Indian continental, there are 49 Akidahs needed to belief which are prescribed in the book of *Bahisctizewah, volume 1,* written by *Mowlarnar Arshif ali Htanewi,* who produced many religious edicts books and recognized him as saint and great spiritual of Taliban sympathizers and Dawah Jamaat. Even though, our educated Muslims point some of their **Akida** are very contradict from the verses of Holy Koran and give the proofs, they accuse the translators of the Holy Koran are deviators of **Akidah or Kaffr (infidels).** Moreover those who study the translation Koran to understand their own language are blamed as "not real Muslims" and exclude from the society.

Most of Muslims' countries and societies have practice enough much closed social tied societies, therefore if someone is evicted from the societies that means it is sanction on him/her. That is why, most of educated Muslims and new generations do not have strength enough against them and they do not have exit to avoid the verses of their Hearsay Koran.

The Holy Koran gives not only fully rights to belief, but also encourage considering, thinking, reminding, meditating and scrutinizing on the Koran. We are never said to follow like blinds.

Do they not then scrutiny on the Koran? (4:82)

And the Holy Koran never says that is someone is going to be killed because of his change faith. The Koran says that whatever he/she does well or bad, he/she is going to achieve its benefit.

We can not be the master of each other among the human being. A person whatever he/she wants, he/she can believe in. If he/she believes wants to be followers of stories or myths, he/she will get his/her own benefit and if he/she believes logically human moral codes, he/she will get his/her benefits too.

Minority Rights in Islam

In any society, there are some misunderstandings between the majority people and minority is naturally. So the strong laws for not to discrimination is essential among human society. The Holy Koran says, there should be honestly, fairly and justice treaty between the majority and minority, and condemns the deceit agreement of majority to betray on minority.

"You make your oaths to be of means of deceit between you because nation is more numerous than another nation." (16: 92)

And then the inner hated (jealous) mind may lead to injustice when decision is made. That basic hate used to exist in the inner minds of people depend on different tribes, sects, religions and past deeds each other. The Holy Koran warns that not to indulge hostile wishes when affairs are made.

"Let not hatred of people incite you not to act equitably; act equitably," (5:8).

However the Holy Koran teaches the laws and human moral code, evil clerics never follow that kind of teaching and ever create the religious edicts (Hearsay Koran) to hostile to others.

Different sects

Therefore, in Muslims countries or Muslims societies, the problems are beyond the natural points between the majority and minority tribe or sects. In somewhere, if there are Sunni Muslims majorities' areas, the other minorities groups such as Shiaa, Khojar, Ebadi or others are under very discrimination. In the same way, in the Shiaa Muslims majorities' areas, the others Muslims sects are under the very discrimination.

Whenever we go to mosques every Friday, we are never lectured how to make peace process, respect and mutual understanding between the different opinion people, but ever inspired to hostile on others and accusing them as infidels which refers to bitter enemies of Islam, not just refers to unbelievers.

Even under the same title "Islam" Sunni and Shiaa acknowledge each other as bitter enemy. The religious edicts of Hearsay Koran clearly proof this point;

> **"Not let to marry Sunni with Shiaa"** *Arlam Giri volume 2, p 264.*

This is very hostile law for followers among the Muslim world. Because-

The Holy Koran says that Muslims are not allowed to marry with bitter enemy in war times (60: 10). Beyond that circumstance, Muslims are not forbidden form marrying with others (5:3).

If so, when we consider above edict from Hearsay Koran "**Not let to marry Sunni with Shiaa**" Arlam Giri volume 2, p 264, that means Sunni and Shiaa are ever bitter enemies each other and they are always in war times compare with the Holy Koran 60:10.

And our so called Islamic governments do not remember to create "peace units or negotiators group" according to the Koran 49: 9, 10 to solve the problem among them.

Non Muslim

"Take counsel with them (non Muslims) in the affairs (3: 159)."

This is very beautiful law of Islam, but it is put only in the Holy Koran and so- called Islamic ruling boards never take it out from the Holy Koran to human's societies. This verse says us in the affairs (ruling, management, legislature, defense) all of State's affairs and every community's affairs we need to take counsel with non Muslims with good attitude. Or non Muslims must involve in the ruling board (administration) in the countries, or communities which are not hundred percent Muslims.

For show or hand-pick minister(s) is illegal or it against the Islamic law because it is not good attitude. Non- Muslim minister(s) has to have rights to defense his/ her/ their representative people.

But now, the lives of non Muslims people of Muslims countries are worse than the people those who belonging to the Islamic title but minority sects. We never think their rights to belief on their own faiths.

Our evil leaders ever teach us that non Muslims are infidels so they are our openly enemies. By pointing the old and wrong page of histories, the evil cleric fabricate many stories about how the non Muslims were plotting to kill our beloved Prophets, destroy to Islam and drive us out from the Islamic prayer places and own lands. Therefore our innocent people are growing up with the anti-non Muslims minded or ever plotting to defeat the non Muslims, because they are threatened that if non Muslims were growing and defeating us they would kill us, drive us out from the own lands and prayer places (mosques). Because we thought the Arabic word *Kuffr* refer to non Muslims.

There are many Muslim people those who personally have good relationship with non Muslims, but most of them are under the heavy criticize. If someone goes to Buddhist Temple, or Church or other religious places, he/she is disgusted in the Islamic Societies.

KUFFR INFIDEL & NON MUSLIM

Even through there are intensely internal fighting among us, we are very untie to hostile on non Muslims. Almost all of we think that all of non Muslims are *Kuffr* (infidels), those who are bitter enemies of Islam and the major plotters to kill our beloved Prophet Muhammad. We know nothing about good thing of *Kuffr* (infidels). We hate or we can not love all of non Muslims whom we have seen or have not seen; justice or injustice, right or wrong.

The major perpetrators of this cause are evil clerics, because they very inspire to the innocent Muslims to hostile on *Kuffr* (infidels) and they blend the *Kuffr* (infidels) with non Muslims, and they cover up what the Holy Koran says about *Kuffr* (infidels) and non Muslims.

What Koran (Islamic laws) says *Kuffr* (infidels)?

All Jews or Christians or those who are not under the title "Islam" are considered as Kuffr (infidels) is the wrong ideology, because the major Kuffr (infidels) came out from own people, not from others.

How they came out?

According to the Holy Koran, people are generally divided into two groups.

   (1) Internal people
   (2) External People

Both internal and external people live together in the same land. But they owned different titles. And those who claim they themselves are Arabs, even though there are multi tribes in them, they are own (internal) people of the Prophet Muhammad and those who they claim they themselves are Jews or Christians even though there are multi tribes in them, they are external people of Prophet Muhammad. Both people are owner of same land and no side can claim who is owner of that land because all of them are native of there.

When Prophet Muhammad started the internal revolution, three different groups came out from own people into-

Muslims (Peace keeper or those who believe in Islamic (peaceful) laws),

Kuffr (Destroyers of peace or those who disbelieve in Islamic (peaceful) laws,) or they cover up the truth or verses of the Holy Koran)

Munafik- Hypocrites (double standers or those who refuge under the title of Islam and setback to Islam).

What the word *Kuffr* stands for

Generally, our clerics let us to understand that the meaning of *Kuffr* is infidel or, but it is not right meaning for *Kuffr* yet.

The Holy Koran itself says

(1)That those whom is invited or explained about the Holy Koran (with understanding language) and if he/she does not accept these laws is Kuffr. (2:26, 8:31)

According to this law, if someone who does not understand about laws of peace (the Holy Koran) yet, how will he/she accept or reject that? We can not make any prejudice those who must be *Kuffr* (infidel) because of their without accepting the Holy Koran before they don't know yet. But they know about the Holy Koran but if they reject to accept the verses of the Holy Koran are called as *Kuffr* (infidels).

There may be very few non Muslim Islamic scholars those who may understand the Koran (but not sure because they might have opportunity to read or study the Hearsay Koran), but many majority of the Non Muslims do not know about the Holy Koran yet. How we can say them as *Kuffr* (infidels)?

Actually, the clerics those who are under the Islamic title are the most well knower about Koran, but they don't accept the verses which are mentions against their cultures or wishes. Why do we dare not to say them as *Kuffr* (infidels)?

(2)That those who understood and really knew about Holy Koran but he/she conceals or covers up or give trouble on the way to truth is Kuffr. (8:19, 36)

The term for *Kuffr* (infidel) for here is very clear, we should not blame to others using this term. Who are responsible to translate to Koran into every language really original sense without Arab's culture exporting? Who are forces to the innocents Muslims to read just Arabic pronunciation that really conceal or cover up the Koran? And who evicts the educated one or activists for human rights according with the Islamic laws that save truth?

Our honestly answer is that our evil clerics are stand on this state. Jews, Christians and other non Muslims are outsiders of this sense. We should bravely consider who infidels are.

(3)That those who understood and really knew about Holy Koran and not only he/she did not accept them but also bitterly fight to Muslims (Peace keeper or those who believe in Islamic (peaceful) laws) is Kuffr. (8: 19)

The word *Kuffr* (infidel) for this term is very important to consider, because this term for *Kuffr* (infidel) is "bitter enemy of Islam" and those who involved in major role to destroy the Islamic faith and plot to kill our Prophet. Today we think that Jews, Christian and other non Muslims ware major enemy of Islam. This is absolutely wrong.

The Holy Koran never say that they are major enemy of Islam, but the Holy Koran clearly says the own people of Prophet Muhammad (in that era, Arab those who against Prophet Muhammad, in this era those who under the title of Islam but against Islam) are *Kuffr* (infidels). We can get this idea from battle of Baddar (Koran Chapter 8) and battle of Uhud (Koran 3: 121 to 154). Who can deny how the infidels (Arabs) were trying to kill our Prophet Muhammad as much as they could?

But today, we entire cover up about infidels Arabs and we believe that only the Jews and Christians are bitter enemies of Islam and we thought that they are same descendants of infidels Arab who were major plotters to kill our Prophet.

Actually, the Jews, Christians and others non Muslims were external people of the era of Prophet Muhammad.

External people

The Arab people were in civil wars, when our Prophet rose out form the Arabs, and he called for peace. He established the peaceful society, abolished the slavery, and revolted for women rights, so he got more and more supporters from the Arabs (his own people) day by day. However his group (Muslims) was bigger, the opponent people were come out from his own people (Arabs), and they started to eradicate the Muslims by using various kind of ways. Under the very serious circumstances, our Prophet sent some of his people to Christians' countries (Abyssinia) to refuge in there.

And in the Mecca, the situation was worse and worse, finally our Prophet himself moved to Medina there multi tribes settled. The Christians of Abyssinia and Jews of Medina did not reject the first Muslims refugees. They were not *Kuffr* infidels (Arabs) who eager to wipe off Muslims.

When the *Kuffr* infidels (Arabs) heard about Muslims community in Medina, their anger were broken out and wished to crush all of Muslims. Therefore they (the Arabs soldiers) marched and fought our Prophet and his followers. But *Kuffr* infidels (Arabs) did not win in the fighting to Muslims. They organized the Jews, Christians and Muslims from Medina to against Prophet Muhammad and his followers, they are human beings and own individual mind, so some of Jews, Christians and Muslims (became *Munarfik*) secretly untied with *Kuffr* infidels (Arabs), but not all of Jews, all of Christians and all of Muslims (Arabs).

In that case, the main organizer were Arabs, and not only some Jews and some Christians supported to infidels Arabs, but also some Muslims (later called them as *Munarfik*) secretly stood on infidels Arabs' side.

In this situation the alliance and the enemy are obviously come out form the people, and when in war times, **we can not take their enemies' alliances (*Kuffr* infidels Arabs, some Jews, some Christians those who are alliances of infidels Arabs) as faithful friends** 5:51, 3:27.

But **not all of Jews or Christians or *Kuffr* infidels are affected this law** (60: 8-9).

But in today, our fellow Muslims are not taught the real historical event and, the teaching of Koran. We are lured to hate Jews, Christians and other non Muslims as like infidels Arabs, the real enemies of Islam (infidels Arabs) are out of senses.

Many of Jews or Christians were supporters of our Prophet Muhammad and his foremost followers (46:10, 5:83). Like these verses are totally covered up and anti Jewish and anti Christian myths are openly created to hide the crimes of infidels Arabs is dishonest.

Religion should be religion, historical event should be historical event, and they should not be mixed each other to cover up the truth. And we should not bring the mood of infidels Arabs to fix up into our new generations' minds hostile on human beings. We should try to create the peace process body and human rights bodies to do the peace among human beings.

OUR FUTURE

Our future is in our hands. If our hands are still closing, we will not free from the bad heritage hand-cuff, still committing the human right abused that against the Holy Koran. So we need to reconsider that-

No non Muslim drive out our women from the mosques, schools, and public involvement. We do these jobs.

Any non Muslim is not the obstacle to learn the Holy Koran with understanding language. But our clerics, our Imams are really obstacles to reach the Holy Koran.

What our deeds affect to us and our reputation is eroding and our human being right is losing because of our behavior or practice. We can not blame on others, and we can not accuse to others in this sense.

We have to open up our brains, thoughts, considerations and aim to human rights and peace process.

We have to throw away **the Hearsay Koran** and we have to take firmly **our Holy Koran**.

Htay Lwin Oo
Islamic Scholar

Citations

Book of –

Arabic Koran

The Translations of Holy Koran

By Dr. Muhammad Taqi-ud-Din al Hilali And Dr. Muhammad Mushin Khan

By Maulvi Muhammad Ali

By Muhammad Marmaduke Pickthall

By A Group of Muslim Brothers & M.H. Shakir

Books of religious edicts (Fatawas), Commentaries & Hadith

Al Meezan

Amdadul Mofthi

Arrlam Giri

Bahistizewar

DorRe Mokhata

Fatawa hi diyat

Haydaya

joultol nira

Kanzuddakaeik

Kuduri

Muartda

Muslim

Shahi Waykaya

Sharmi

Whashkath